LET'S THINK ABOUT

Animal Rights

Vic Parker

Raintree is an imprint of Capstone Global Library Limited, a company incorporated in England and Wales having its registered office at 7 Pilgrim Street, London, EC4V 6LB – Registered company number: 6695582

www.raintreepublishers.co.uk
myorders@raintreepublishers.co.uk

Edited by John Paul Wilkins, Clare Lewis, and Kathryn Clay
Designed by Tim Bond and Peggie Carley
Picture research by Liz Alexander and Tracy Cummins
Production by Victoria Fitzgerald
Originated by Capstone Global Library Ltd
Printed and bound in China by CTPS

ISBN 978 1 406 28263 4
18 17 16 15 14
10 9 8 7 6 5 4 3 2 1

British Library Cataloguing in Publication Data
A full catalogue record for this book is available from the British Library.

Acknowledgements
We would like to thank the following for permission to reproduce photographs:
Alamy: © Adrian Sherratt, 12, © Angela Hampton Picture Library, 32, © Carolyn Jenkins, 18, © Robert Harding Picture Library Ltd, 22, 23; Corbis: © Cliff Hide/Demotix, 39, © Cyril Ruoso/ JH Editorial/Minden Pictures, 9, © Daniel J. Cox, 7, © Pallava Bagla, 15, © Simon Lim/Visuals Unlimited, 28, © Ted Wood/Aurora Photos, 5; Cruelty Free International: (Leaping Bunny logo is a registered trademark of Cruelty Free International), 17; Getty Images: De Agostini, 4, Jahi Chikwendiu/The Washington Post, 16, James Devaney/WireImage, 10, JEREMY SUTTON-HIBBERT, 40, Monaco Centre de Presse-pool, 33, Muammer Mujdat Uzel, front cover, Slaven Vlasic, 30, 31; Shutterstock: Alexander Mak, 26, Dobermaraner, 8, EcoPrint, 36, Featureflash, 13, Kletr, 25, polat, 21, spflaum, 20, Stayer, 35, Yurchyks, 14; U.S. Navy photo: Photographer's Mate 1st Class Brien Aho, 11.

Every effort has been made to contact copyright holders of material reproduced in this book. Any omissions will be rectified in subsequent printings if notice is given to the publisher.

Contents

Animal rights: what's the issue?. 4

What are animal rights? 6

Using animals in scientific research 12

Animals as food: what are the issues? 18

Using animals in the fashion industry 26

Using animals for sport and entertainment 32

The animal rights movement: how far is reasonable? 38

The future of animal rights 42

Debate it!. 44

Glossary 45

Find out more. 46

Index 48

Some words are shown in bold, **like this**.
You can find out what they mean by looking in the glossary.

Animal rights: what's the issue?

In ancient times people didn't have supermarkets and shopping precincts. They had to hunt for the clothing and food they needed. Over time they began using animals to help make farming and other work easier. People also began keeping animals as companions and using them in sports and entertainment. But today people have access to equipment and other food and clothing sources. Some people have begun to question whether it is right for humans to use animals in these ways.

Animal welfare

Today many people think it is acceptable to use animals to meet our needs, as long as they are looked after and do not suffer unnecessarily. This viewpoint is known as animal welfare. Many countries have passed animal welfare laws. The laws aim to ensure that animals are given an appropriate environment in which they can display normal behaviour patterns, have sufficient food, and are protected from injury and disease.

This Roman mosaic shows cockfighting, a sport that goes back 6,000 years to ancient Persia. Cockfighting is a controversial activity because it makes chickens fight to the death.

Animal rights

Some people argue that providing basic needs to animals is not enough. These people say that animals should have **rights** to these things. They say that we should provide them even if humans end up worse off for doing so. This viewpoint is known as animal rights. So how should we treat animals? Read on to make up your mind.

DID YOU KNOW?

The modern idea of animal rights began in the 1970s. Richard D. Ryder argued that it is wrong for humans to think they are better than animals. The idea was popularized by a 1975 book called *Animal Liberation* by Peter Singer. Singer's book triggered the formation of animal rights organizations around the world.

Elephants in Crisis is an organization that rescues elephants put to work in Asia.

What are animal rights?

Every one of us has human rights. These are basic standards of life that every person deserves, no matter who or where they are. These rights allow everyone to exist in a world that is fair and just. They include the right to live free and the right to have food and a home somewhere safe. Other rights include the right to be treated equally and the right to think and express yourself as you want.

Human rights were first listed in a document called the Universal Declaration of Human Rights. It was drawn up by representatives from many countries in 1948 after World War II ended. Since then many countries have passed laws to protect human rights.

A Universal Declaration of Animal Rights was drawn up in 1978 by animal rights groups meeting at the United Nations' Educational, Scientific and Cultural Organization (UNESCO). However, it did not gain widespread international support because people cannot agree on what rights animals should have.

WHAT DO YOU THINK?

If laws were passed that gave animals basic rights, rearing or hunting animals for food or clothes would become illegal. It would be illegal to perform scientific experiments on animals. Even killing "pests" in your home such as wasps or mice would be illegal. Zoos, marine parks and conservation programmes would all have to close. You would not be allowed to keep animals as pets. Do you agree with this idea?

Humans are cutting down the bamboo forests that are home to giant pandas. Should animals have the right to live without humans destroying their habitats?

Why should animals have rights?

People argue that animals should have rights because many can feel pleasure and pain. This ability is called sentience. Since ancient times people have observed that a cat purrs contentedly when it is stroked, and a dog yelps in pain if it is kicked. Some animals display "clever" behaviour, such as birds building complicated nests. However, people assumed these were physical reactions or **instinctive behaviour** that does not involving complex emotions, thought patterns, or problem solving and learning. It has also been argued that sentience belongs only to certain types of animals with large brains, such as mammals.

For the past 100 years people have studied animal sentience as a science. It has become widely accepted that many more animals can feel pleasure and pain than was once thought. This list includes all **vertebrates**, some **invertebrates** and some **crustaceans**. There is scientific evidence to show that animals are capable of levels of awareness, emotion, relationship-building and intelligence similar to humans.

Dr. Irene Pepperberg's research with captive African grey parrots shows that they have intelligence similar to human toddlers. The parrots are able to recognize shapes, colours and numbers.

Can animals grieve?

University professor and science award winner Marc Bekoff once said, "Grieving and mourning clearly show that non-human animals are socially aware of what is happening in their worlds and that they feel deep emotions when family and friends die." Does this affect how you feel about rights for animals?

Chimpanzees are able to recognize themselves in a mirror.

What is animal cruelty?

Some people say that animals should be granted rights purely because they can feel pain. British **philosopher** Jeremy Bentham (1748–1832) said, "The question is not 'Can they reason?' nor 'Can they talk?' but 'Can they suffer?'"

The **Humane** Society of the United States defines animal cruelty as "either deliberate abuse or simply the failure to take care of an animal". However, while some instances of animal cruelty are obvious, others may not be as easy to identify. For example, is dressing up a dog harmless or harmful?

Paris Hilton has been accused of treating animals as fashion accessories.

Is it cruel to keep animals as pets or make animals work for us, even if they are well loved and looked after? Some animal rights supporters would say that a guide dog suffers if you train it to assist a blind person. Even though the dog has been bred as a domestic animal and is well cared for, it is not free to live a natural life.

The US Army trains dolphins for use in wartime to detect and clear underwater mines at sea. Is this animal cruelty? If so, is it justifiable if it saves human lives?

Using animals in scientific research

Each year millions of animals around the world are used in scientific experiments. Many of these experiments are carried out in attempts to find cures and treatments for diseases. Many other animal experiments are to test make-up, toiletries and household products to satisfy tough safety laws.

Animal experiments can take many forms. Animals may be infected with illnesses or undergo surgery. Or they may be used to test poisonous substances. **Anaesthetics** are not always used because this may affect the test results. Some animals become ill after the tests and have to be killed.

Animal rights supporters claim that research and testing using animals is extremely cruel and either unnecessary or of little value. They want to end all animal experimentation, which they call **vivisection.**

Animal rights supporters often protest against animal experimentation.

Banning animal testing

Due to animal rights **campaigns**, in 2013 the European Union banned the selling of make-up and toiletries that have involved any testing on animals. However, there is no such ban in the United States or Canada. There is no ban anywhere for the sale of household cleaning products tested on animals. Many governments actively support animal experimentation for medical purposes and consider it essential research.

Leona Lewis serves as a brand **activist** for The Body Shop, a company that sells make-up and other toiletries.

WHAT DO YOU THINK?

Is research on animals justifiable, or should it be outlawed?

Animal research

Universities, medical schools, pharmaceutical companies and the military all experiment on animals. Most countries have laws aimed at controlling how many times individual animals may be used, the numbers of animals used, and the level of pain involved. However, each country has different laws. In the United States, mice, rats, birds, reptiles and amphibians have little legal protection. These animals are not included in the Animal Welfare Act. Some experts believe that these creatures make up 90 percent of the estimated 26 million animals used in US labs. Mice make up a large majority. In 2012 the UK performed 4.1 million animal experiments. Of these, 74 percent were performed on mice. No experiments were carried out on gorillas, orangutans or chimpanzees. Fewer than 0.2 percent of experiments involved monkeys, dogs or cats.

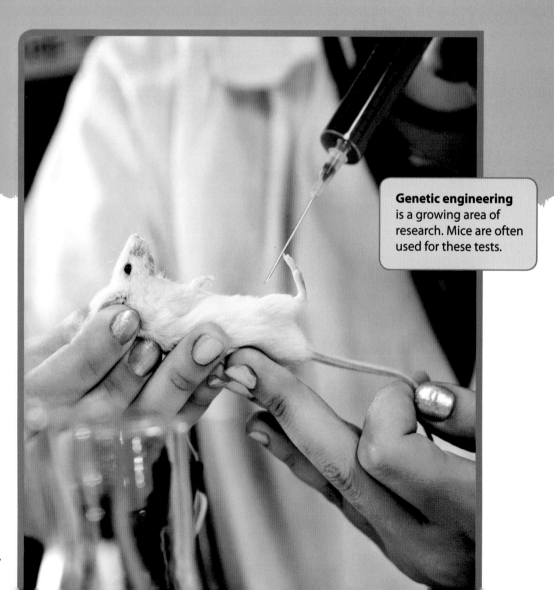

Genetic engineering is a growing area of research. Mice are often used for these tests.

Scientists claim that experiments on primates are important. Scientists use primates to research brain illnesses and to test the safety of new drugs, such as cancer treatments.

Controversy over conditions in labs

Animal rights activists describe dreadful living conditions for creatures in laboratories. However, scientists claim they look after animals carefully. The scientists argue that stress causes changes in animals' bodies, which would alter the results of experiments. So their goal is to keep animals as happy as possible.

Why use animals in research?

People who support medical research on animals claim the testing is essential to find out whether a medicine is safe for human trials. They say many life-saving breakthroughs would not have happened without animal testing. Vaccinations, organ transplants, open-heart surgery, insulin treatment for diabetes and cancer drugs were all tested using animals.

Some classrooms have replaced real frog dissections with computer simulations.

DID YOU KNOW?

Scientists who experiment on animals follow a principle suggested by two researchers in the 1950s called "the three Rs". They REPLACE animals with alternative techniques where possible. They REDUCE the numbers of animals to a minimum. They REFINE the way experiments are performed so that animals suffer as little as possible.

Alternatives to animal testing

Animal rights supporters disagree that medical advances are due to experiments on animals. They argue that animals rarely serve as good models for the human body. For example, in the 1950s and 1960s the drug Thalidomide was tested on animals and passed for use by humans. Later it was found to cause babies to be born with deformities. Animal rights supporters claim that testing on human cells or by computer models takes less time to complete, is cheaper and can be more accurate. However, scientists argue that nothing can substitute testing on a living creature.

Cosmetics and household products that have the Leaping Bunny logo are guaranteed free from animal testing.

Animals as food: what are the issues?

People have eaten animals and animal products such as eggs, dairy and honey for thousands of years. Many people say this is natural and that plenty of animals eat other animals. People also claim it is good for health. For example, vitamin B12 is vital for red blood cells and nerves. B12 is found mainly in meat, fish, eggs and milk. Oily fish contains omega-3 fatty acids, which protect against heart disease.

Some countries have food labelling laws that enable people to see which foods do not contain meat or fish.

Food choices

Many animal rights supporters choose to be vegetarian or vegan. A vegetarian does not eat meat or fish. A vegan does not eat meat, fish or animal products such as eggs or cheese. Animal rights supporters argue that it is wrong to rear animals so we can eat them. They also say we can be healthy eating a plant-based diet. For instance, vitamin B12 is in fortified veggie burgers and soy products. Omega-3 is in flax seed oil. Some claim that a diet of animal products is actually unhealthy because eating fatty meats can lead to heart disease.

DID YOU KNOW?

Famous vegetarians include Leona Lewis, Christian Bale, Natalie Portman and Russell Brand. Famous vegans include Bill Clinton, Lea Michele, Carrie Underwood and Ellen DeGeneres.

Intensive farming or factory farming?

One reason animal rights supporters argue for vegetarianism and veganism is because they claim that some farming methods are cruel. One type of modern farming raises large numbers of animals in small spaces using low-quality animal feed and drugs to make the animals grow faster. The method is known as intensive farming. Supporters say that it is the most efficient way to produce food. They claim that it is the only way farmers can produce enough low-cost food for the world's rapidly growing population. It also allows the shipping of food to countries that cannot produce enough of their own.

On some egg farms hens live in cages with wire floors. Some people say the wire floors hurt the hens' feet.

Animal rights supporters call this process "factory farming". They claim it prevents animals from having a natural life and causes them suffering. For instance, on some egg farms thousands of hens are crammed into small cages and kept in huge sheds. Their beaks are often trimmed down so they don't peck each other. On intensive dairy farms, cows give birth every year and are then given drugs so they produce about four times as much milk as is natural. The cows can only keep producing such large quantities for about four or five years. Afterward, they are killed.

Intensive farm owners say that they operate within their country's animal welfare laws. They do not consider their practices to be animal cruelty.

Milking sheds on intensive farms can be cramped. Cows have no room to move freely.

DID YOU KNOW?

In the United States, intensive farms are called animal feeding operations (AFOs) or confined animal feeding operations (CAFOs). According to the 2002 Census of Agriculture, intensive farming accounts for more than 99 percent of all farmed animals in the United States.

Farming affordable meat

Animals most often raised for meat on intensive farms include chickens, pigs and beef cows. Intensive farms use methods that produce as much food as possible, as cheaply as possible. Doing so allows thousands of people to eat meat who wouldn't otherwise be able to afford it. Many experts claim this is important for health. Hugh Pennington, a Scottish university professor, said, "Prior to the 1950s, large numbers of people died because of tuberculosis due to a simple lack of nourishment. The wide availability of cheap animal proteins … has put an end to that."

Animal rights supporters do not agree that eating meat brings health benefits. They also claim that animal welfare laws do not go far enough to protect animals on intensive farms from suffering due to unnatural conditions. For instance, chickens are reared in large windowless sheds packed with thousands of birds. They are bred to grow twice as fast as normal. Pigs are kept indoors in crowded sheds that have concrete or slatted floors with no bedding.

Over-use of antibiotics?

Scientists warn that some antibiotics used to treat infections in humans are becoming resistant to germs. This means that in the future, diseases we can currently cure might kill us. Intensive farmers use large quantities of antibiotics to prevent or treat disease in their animals. However, this might not be in the best interest of humans long-term. According to the charity Compassion in World Farming, "Although resistance in human infections is mainly caused by human antibiotic use … farm-animal use contributes significantly."

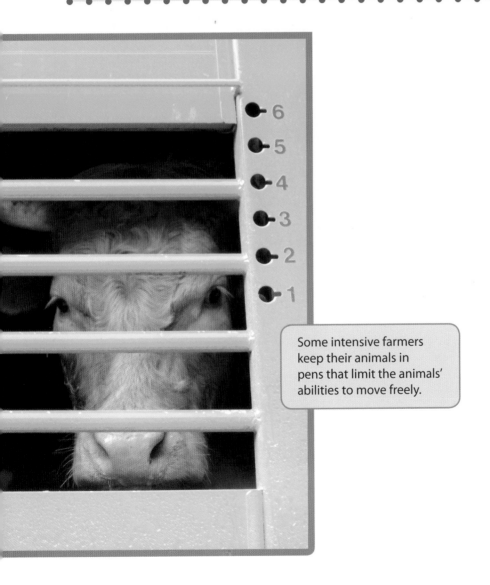

Some intensive farmers keep their animals in pens that limit the animals' abilities to move freely.

Are there intensive farms for fish?

We are eating more fish than ever before. This is partly because many experts say we should, as fish is a good source of protein, vitamins and minerals. Demand has caused too much fishing, so wild fish stocks have run dangerously low. Some species, such as Atlantic bluefin tuna, have become endangered. This harms the balance of life in the oceans and also impacts people who make a living from fishing. To avoid completely wiping out wild fish species, fish farms were created to breed fish to meet the popular demand. Fish farms now breed about 50 percent of the world's fish for consumption.

Animal rights supporters claim that fish farming is cruel. They say increasing scientific evidence suggests that fish are complex creatures that can feel pain, fear and stress. Fish bred on farms live in crowded enclosures which results in injuries and infections. The fish produce so much waste that it causes water pollution problems. Animal rights supporters claim that slaughter laws do not go far enough to protect fish from distress and pain.

Alternatives to intensive farming

Some animal welfare supporters prefer free-range farming that allows animals outdoor space to live as naturally as possible. They also support organic farming, which does not involve the use of drugs. Intensive farmers argue that these methods often do not protect animals from injury and illness. They say free-range and organic farming could not supply enough food to feed the world. What do you think?

Fish farms can be land-based, where fish are bred in tanks or ponds. They can also be sea-based, where fish are bred in cages near the shore. The fish above are being reared in a land-based fish farm.

Using animals in the fashion industry

Animal products have been used as clothes since prehistoric times, when humans kept warm in skins and furs. Wool has been made into clothing for about 12,000 years. Silk made from silk worms' cocoon threads was first produced in China more than 4,500 years ago.

Production of the plant-based fabric linen has thrived in Europe since medieval times. The plant-based fabric cotton has been mass-produced in the UK and United States since the 1800s. Many synthetic, or human-made, fabrics such as nylon and polyester were developed during the 1900s. Animal rights supporters argue that it is no longer necessary to use animals for clothing. They also claim that many animals are treated cruelly to supply the needs of the fashion industry.

Millions of wild kangaroos are killed each year in Australia for skin to make football boots.

Leather and skins

Most leather is made from cows. Other kinds of leather come from animals bred especially for their skins. Skin is the main value of ostriches farmed in South Africa and alligators farmed in the United States. Their meat is sold as a by-product.

Animal rights supporters say that pigs, goats, sheep, horses, snakes, and lizards are all killed for their skins in parts of the world that have very limited animal welfare laws or none at all.

WHAT DO YOU THINK?

There are many synthetic alternatives to leather that look just like the real thing. In 2006 football star David Beckham switched to synthetic leather shoes. Would you prefer synthetic leather shoes or ones made of leather?

Fur farming

Animal rights supporters agree that animals should not be killed for their fur. About 85 percent of the fur industry's skins come from animals on fur farms. These are places where animals such as mink, foxes, chinchillas and rabbits are bred especially for their pelts. Animal rights supporters argue that the animals live miserable lives in cramped cages and suffer painful deaths. More than 30 million animals are killed on fur farms each year.

The International Fur Trade Federation (IFTF) claims that fur farms are careful to consider the animals' welfare. The group says it spends millions of dollars on research and technology to support animal welfare. The IFTF argues that fur farming is more environmentally friendly than the production of synthetic fur. The group also says that fur farming provides employment for thousands of people in Europe and North America.

Mink bred for their fur are transported in small cages.

WHAT DO YOU THINK?

Celebrities such as Lady Gaga and Kanye West have been criticized for wearing fur. Just like leather, there are many alternatives to fur that look and feel like the real thing. Would you prefer a fake fur coat or one made of real fur?

Wild fur

Most of the fashion industry's wild fur comes from Russia, Canada, and the United States. People who support the killing of wild animals for fur claim that many small, rural communities rely on hunting for income. They also claim that it can be necessary for the sake of other wildlife to **cull** animals that threaten to overrun a particular habitat.

Scientists who have inspected culling have stated that methods such as clubbing are "acceptably humane" and compare favourably with methods used in slaughterhouses. However, animal rights supporters disagree. They say that culling methods are unacceptably violent. They also point out that in trapping, animals can suffer for days before dying.

What's wrong with wool?

According to The Campaign for Wool, wool is "warmer in winter but cooler in summer; it holds its shape better than synthetics and it's longer-lasting …" The Campaign also claims that wool is more environmentally friendly than fabrics produced using chemicals in factories.

However, animal rights supporters disagree. They claim that farming sheep for wool is cruel. They argue that flocks of thousands are so large that diseases spread quickly. They say sheep shearers work so fast they handle sheep roughly and sometimes injure them. Some sheep are sheared too soon in spring and die of cold. Others are sent to slaughterhouses when their wool production declines.

What is the future for fashion?

Some designers do not believe they should avoid using animals. Many fashion companies actively support the use of natural fibres from animals or plants as a "greener" choice that is better for the planet than synthetic fabrics.

However, fashion companies are also mindful that an increasing number of people think that using animals for clothing is unacceptable. They aim to use a wide range of synthetic materials as well as animal-based textiles. They also make labelling clear so it is easy for customers to choose what they want to buy.

The international fur trade does not use endangered species for clothing. However, fur from endangered species is sometimes sold illegally. Animals affected include tigers, leopards, snow leopards, jaguars, ocelots, river otters and platypuses.

Fashion designer Stella McCartney (second from right), a vegetarian, does not use leather or fur in her creations.

Using animals for sport and entertainment

Many animals are featured in shows or sports. People concerned with animal welfare say it is only wrong to keep animals for entertainment if they have a lower quality of life than they would in the wild. However, animal rights supporters argue that it is always wrong for humans to make animals perform in shows or use them for sport.

Some forms of entertainment aim to teach humans about animals.

Animal performers

Animal rights activists insist that animals should not be taught to perform tricks in circuses or on TV and in films. They argue that it is degrading and humiliating to the animals. They are also concerned that cruel training methods are often used. Due to awareness campaigns, many circuses now only feature human performers. Many TV and film companies employ animal welfare experts to make sure they use only animal performers that are well treated. They are careful not to harm any animals during filming.

However, animal rights supporters claim that with the availability of computerized special effects, there is little need to use animals in TV and films at all.

Doggy dancing and other forms of dog agility are popular with many people.

WHAT DO YOU THINK?

Are forms of dog agility cruel and humiliating to the animals? Or is it a way of showing off the loving bond between dogs and their owners, and how clever the animals are?

Captivity or conservation?

Millions of people enjoy going to see animals in zoos, safari parks, marine parks and aquariums. Supporters of animal parks claim that they play an important role in educating people about animals, which encourages us to protect animals. Many animal parks also give endangered species a safe place to breed. At the parks the animals are protected from poachers, predators and habitat loss, which is vital to keep them from extinction. Many safari parks also fund conservation programmes, which do important work to save threatened animals in the wild.

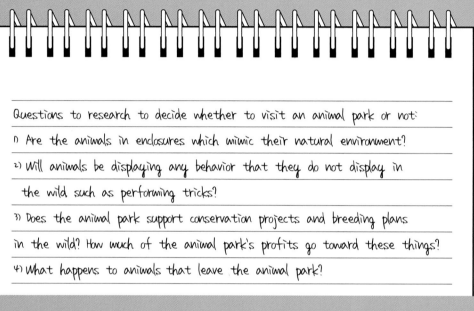

Questions to research to decide whether to visit an animal park or not:

1) Are the animals in enclosures which mimic their natural environment?

2) Will animals be displaying any behavior that they do not display in the wild such as performing tricks?

3) Does the animal park support conservation projects and breeding plans in the wild? How much of the animal park's profits go toward these things?

4) What happens to animals that leave the animal park?

Considerations to make before visiting an animal park

Animal shelters and sanctuaries

Animal shelters are sometimes criticized. Even though they look after and rehome unwanted animals, this often means keeping animals in confined spaces for long periods of time. Animal rights supporters prefer animal sanctuaries. These are facilities where unwanted animals or injured wildlife can live for the rest of their lives. The animals are given the opportunity to behave as naturally as possible in a protective environment. Do you think animals should be placed in shelters and eventually re-homed or moved to animal sanctuaries?

Animal rights supporters argue that people do not have the right to capture, confine and breed other animals – even if they are endangered. They criticize animal and safari parks for existing mainly to entertain people, with breeding and conservation programmes only a secondary concern. Animal rights supporters argue that many animal parks are only interested in breeding the most popular species, such as big cats. They claim that animal parks buy and sell creatures like objects. They are also concerned that animal parks sometimes keep animals in very poor conditions and that an animal's natural behaviour is severely restricted even in well-run parks.

Polar bears born and raised in captivity are rarely released back into the wild.

Animals in sport

Animals have been used for sport since the ancient Greeks and Romans used horses for chariot racing. Animal welfare supporters claim it is acceptable to use animals in sport as long as they are well treated. Animal rights activists argue that any use of animals in sport is wrong. Horse racing and dog racing are among their main concerns. They say that people train animals for these activities just to gamble money. They claim that racing can be harmful. Dogs can suffer injuries from continually running around tight-cornered tracks. Horses can be injured going over high jumps.

Greyhounds are a popular breed used for dog racing.

Hunting and fishing

Hunting and fishing are also ancient, worldwide sports. Many people say that hunting is necessary to help control the numbers of certain animals, such as foxes and deer. Animal rights supporters argue that there are more humane ways of controlling animal populations and that hunting is just animal cruelty for human enjoyment. Animal rights supporters claim that fishing is also cruel. They argue that even the smallest fish has the ability to feel stress and pain, so even catching fish and releasing them back into the water is torture.

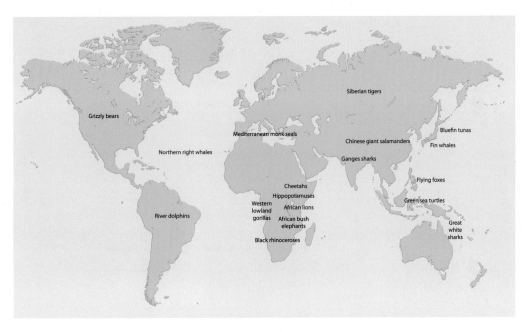

Species under the threat of extinction from overhunting

The animal rights movement: how far is reasonable?

Most people concerned with animal rights stand up for their beliefs in moderate ways. They might sign petitions, write to local newspapers or politicians, go on peaceful protest marches and raise money for animal protection organizations and campaigns. Many people simply refuse to use companies and products that they believe harm animals. This is called boycotting. For instance, some people refuse to buy products from intensive farms and companies that test their products on animals. Other people refuse to visit zoos and marine parks.

Exposing and educating

A few animal rights supporters have gone undercover to investigate and expose cruelty to animals. Such people were hired at medical research laboratories and intensive farms. Then they secretly filmed and photographed cases of poor treatment. As a result of secret investigations, certain people responsible for particular cases of cruelty have been made to stop. Animal rights supporters have also used the investigations as the basis for long-term worldwide animal rights campaigns.

DID YOU KNOW?

Some animal rights supporters decide to carry out undercover investigations on their own. However, a few organizations actually advertise jobs for animal rights undercover agents and give people training. One such organization is People for the Ethical Treatment of Animals (PETA).

Animal rights supporters participate in peaceful protests against the cruel treatment of animals.

Direct action

A few animal rights supporters believe in taking direct action. For instance, fox hunt **saboteurs** attempt to delay and confuse the horses and hounds belonging to riders who are chasing a fox. Doing so gives a fox more time to escape.

Most animal rights supporters who take direct action are careful to keep within the law. For instance, Sea Shepherd is an organization in the United States that seeks to stop illegal **whaling**. The members sail a small fleet of boats to chase whalers and get in the way of crews harpooning the creatures.

Activisits who disagree with the hunting of whales and dolphins sometimes take their protests to the seas.

Extreme action

A few animal rights supporters believe that any action they take can be justified, even if it is illegal. Animal rights supporters have graffitied and vandalized buildings where they believe animal abuse happens. They have **trespassed** into laboratories, fur farms and slaughterhouses. They have wrecked equipment and freed animals. They have harassed people whom they believe work in jobs involving animal cruelty by sending abusive letters, making threatening phone calls, and demonstrating outside their homes. A tiny number of activists have actually attacked people or set fire to their buildings and cars. Animal rights supporters like these are prepared to go to prison for their beliefs – and some have.

WHAT DO YOU THINK?

In the United States a few animal rights groups have been officially listed as **terrorist** organizations. However, the people involved would say that they are animal freedom fighters. When do you think direct action crosses the line and becomes terrorism?

The future of animal rights

The issue of animal rights raises important questions about our place in the universe and our own rights and responsibilities to the world around us. There is no agreed upon answer to the question "should animals have rights?"

In recent years laws and guidelines have been put in place that aim to protect animals from cruelty. However, animal rights supporters say these laws do not go far enough. Many people believe that serious and widespread animal cruelty issues still exist. Other people say the practices are necessary to feed the world.

Where to go from here?

The animal rights movement has come a long way since its rise in the 1970s. Today animal rights is a major discussion topic in schools and courtrooms. It is a debate that will carry on for years to come.

WHAT DO YOU THINK?

If you could write a worldwide **charter** for animal rights, similar to the Universal Declaration of Human Rights, what would you list in it?

Animal Rights Legislation

Some states, countries, and regions have their own laws to protect animals. But there are no worldwide treaties for animal welfare or animal rights.

Treaties that have been proposed, but not adopted are:
• The Universal Declaration of Animal Rights (drawn up in 1978)

• The International Convention for the Protection of Animals (drawn up in 1988)

• The Universal Declaration of Animal Welfare (drawn up in 2003, redrafted in 2005 and 2011)

Debate it!

Are you ready to debate some of these issues with your friends?
If so, these five tips may help.

1. Be prepared. Do some research before you begin. Make a list of points you plan to debate. Then think of arguments on the other side. Then you'll be prepared when your friend mentions them.

2. State your opinions clearly. It's useful to provide examples and statistics.

3. Listen carefully. After all, you cannot respond effectively unless you understand exactly what your friend is saying. You can ask your friend to repeat the comment or provide further information.

4. Keep your cool. In a good debate, there is no clear winner or loser. You will win some points and lose others. You may even find that some of your friend's comments make sense. That's not bad. It shows that you are keeping an open mind.

5. Have fun! Debate is a great way to explore the issues.

Glossary

activist person who works for social or political change

agility ability to move in a quick and easy way

anaesthetic substance that reduces sensitivity to pain, sometimes with loss of consciousness

campaign organized actions and events with a specific goal, such as being elected

charter official document granting permission to set up a new organization or company

conservation protection of animals and plants, as well as the wise use of what we get from nature

crustacean sea animal with an outer skeleton, such as a crab, lobster or shrimp

cull kill the weak, sick and old animals in a herd

genetic engineering inserting genes from one species into the chromosomes of another species

humane kind, with mercy

instinctive behaviour behaviour that is natural rather than learned

invertebrate animal without a backbone

philosopher person who studies ideas, the way people think and the search for knowledge

right moral or legal gurantee to something

saboteur person who damages, destroys or disrupts on purpose

terrorist person who uses threats or force to frighten or harm others

trespass enter someone's private property without permission

vertebrate animal with a backbone

vivisection cutting open of a living creature to study how its body functions

whaling hunting whales for their meat, oil and bones

Find out more

Books

Animal Rights (Introducing Issues With Opposing Viewpoints), Lauri S. Friedman
(Greenhaven Press, 2011)

Animal Rights: How You Can Make a Difference (Take Action),
Rhonda Lucas Donald (Snap Books, 2009)

Animal Rights: What Everyone Needs to Know, Paul Waldau
(Oxford University Press, 2011)

Zoos and Animal Welfare (Issues that Concern You), Christine van Tuyl
(Greenhaven Press, 2008)

Websites

www.rspca.org.uk/allaboutanimals/laboratory
Visit the RSPC website to learn more about the issues surrounding animal welfare,
and the organization's views on the treatment of laboratory animals.

www.dosomething.org/cause/animals
Learn how you can make a difference in animal welfare.

www.worldwildlife.org
Read about the issues affecting wildlife all over the world, and learn ways that
you can help animals and wildlife.

Further research

Do some further research on the current treatment of animals and the history of animal rights. Consider the following topics:
- animals and the science classroom
- animal shelters
- wildlife

When researching animals in the science classroom, first consider your own school's policies. Are animals dissected at your school? Find out why or why not. Interview science teachers, science students, and other school officials. Are there alternative choices your school could utilize?

When researching animal shelters, try to visit local shelters in your community. Who sponsors the shelter? How are animals treated there? How could the treatment of local shelter animals be improved?

When researching wildlife, consider the wild animals that live in your state or region. Are any of these animals endangered? If so, what steps are being taken to protect them? What could you do to help these animals?

Index

activists 15, 36, 40, 41

animal cruelty 10, 12, 20, 24,
    33, 38, 41, 41

animal research 14, 16

animal rights 5, 6, 38, 42, 43

animal testing 12, 13, 14, 16, 17, 38

animal welfare 4, 43

captivity 34, 35

conservation 34, 35

education 34, 38

entertainment 32, 33, 34, 35

farming 4, 6, 20, 21, 22, 23, 24,
    25, 38, 41

fashion industry 26, 28, 29, 30

fishing 24, 37

food 4, 6, 18, 19, 20, 21, 22

fur industry 26, 28, 29, 30, 31, 41

human rights 6, 42

hunting 4, 6, 29, 37

instinctive behaviour 8

pets 10, 11

sanctuaries 34, 35

scientific experiments 6, 12, 15, 16, 17

sentience 8, 9

shelters 34

sports 26, 27, 32, 36, 37

vegans 19, 20

vegetarians 19, 20

whaling 40

wool 30